Great for phonics
and vocabulary
development.

40 Reproducible
Word Ladders

Pirate
Word
Ladders

by Brenda Olsen

3rd
grade

Printed in the United States of America

First Printing, 2012

ISBN-13: 978-1492216308
ISBN-10: 1492216305

www.kayedstudio.com

Word Ladders

In this book you will find 40 reproducible *Pirate word ladders*. These word ladders are a great way for students to analyze words and will help students with decoding, spelling, and vocabulary development.

Using Word Ladders
Students will start at the bottom of the word ladder and use the directions and clues to create new words as they move to the top of each word ladder.

Example
The word ladder starts with the word *Jack*. The directions tell you to change the first letter and the clue is, "Put your homework in your back_____." The word that you need to make is *pack*.

More Ideas

Allow students to work on the word ladders in pairs.

You can always come up with more clues if students get stuck.

Some of the ladders will also be great to use as word sorts. Allowing students to look for patterns in words.

Name: _____

Pirate Word Ladders

Directions - Read the clues and write each word on the ladder. Start at the bottom and climb to the top of the ladder.

team

Change the last letter. (a group working toward the same goal)

tear

Change the first letter. (comes out of your eyes when crying)

fear

Change the first letter. (when you feel scared)

pear

Change the last letter. (a fruit)

peak

Remove the first two letters and add one to the beginning. (the top of a mountain)

sneak

Remove 3 letters. (to move around in a secret way)

sneakers

Pirate Word Ladders

Directions - Read the clues and write each word on the ladder. Start at the bottom and climb to the top of the ladder.

string

Add one letter. (Cats like to play with balls of _____.)

sting

Change the second letter. (I'm afraid the bee will _____ me.)

sling

Change the first letter. (A _____-shot allows you to throw rocks long distances.)

cling

Change the "h" to an "l" and add a letter at the end. (to hold on tightly)

chin

Remove the last two letters and add one to the end. (the part of the face below the mouth)

chick

Remove 2 letters. (a baby chicken)

chicken

Name: _____

Pirate Word Ladders

Directions - Read the clues and write each word on the ladder. Start at the bottom and climb to the top of the ladder.

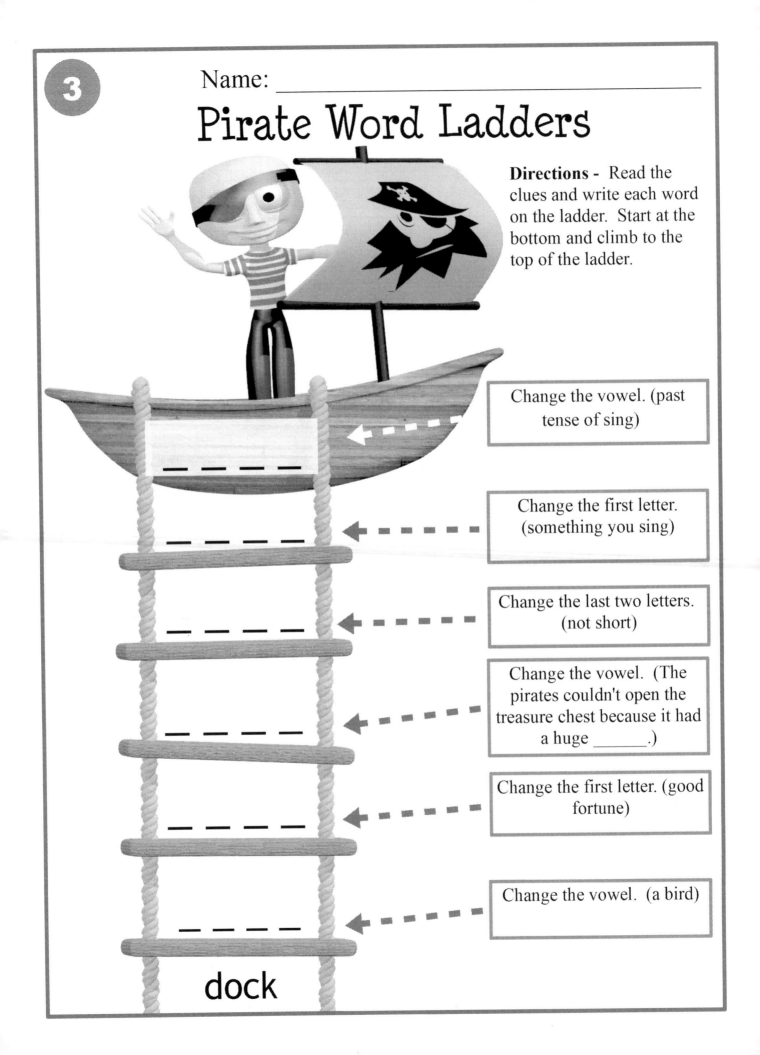

_ _ _ _

Change the vowel. (past tense of sing)

_ _ _ _

Change the first letter. (something you sing)

_ _ _ _

Change the last two letters. (not short)

_ _ _ _

Change the vowel. (The pirates couldn't open the treasure chest because it had a huge _____.)

_ _ _ _

Change the first letter. (good fortune)

_ _ _ _

Change the vowel. (a bird)

dock

Pirate Word Ladders

Directions - Read the clues and write each word on the ladder. Start at the bottom and climb to the top of the ladder.

_ _ _ _

_ _ _ _

_ _ _ _

_ _ _ _

_ _ _ _ _

replace

Change the vowel. (something to eat)

Change one letter. (a contest)

Change the first letter. (very angry)

Remove the "p" and change the "c." (a wise person or a spice)

Remove the "l" and add a letter at the beginning. (Aliens are coming from outer _____.)

Remove the first 2 letters. (Robin got first _____ in the science fair.)

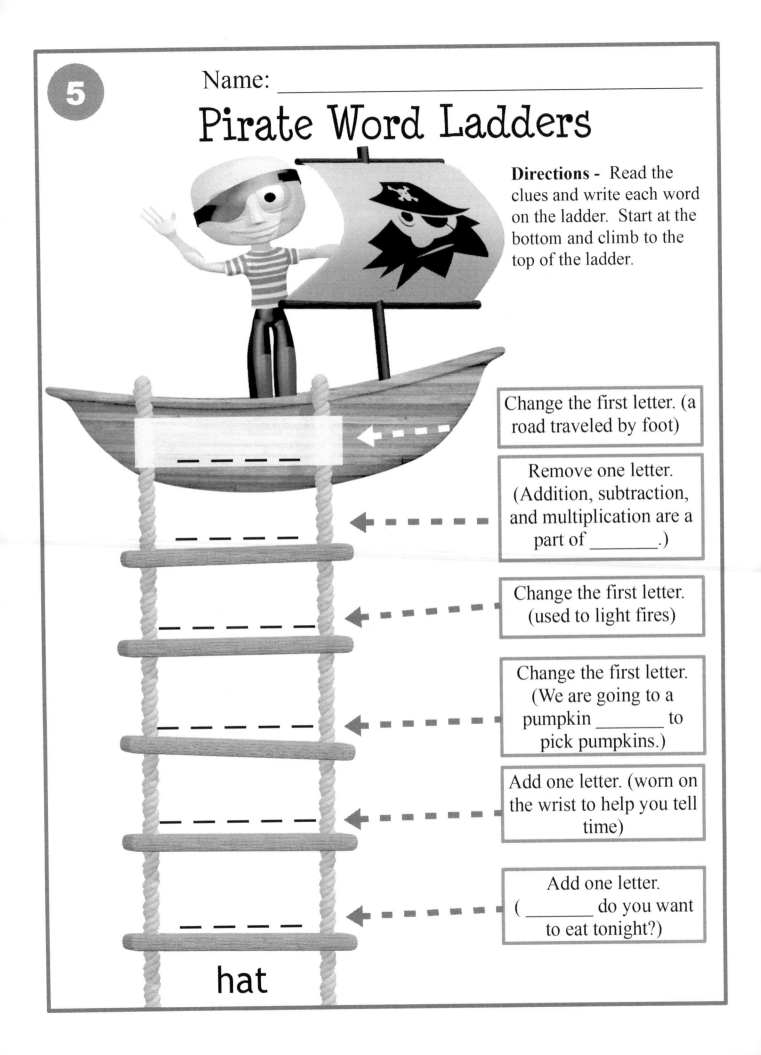

Name: _____

Pirate Word Ladders

Directions - Read the clues and write each word on the ladder. Start at the bottom and climb to the top of the ladder.

_ _ _ _ _

Change the first letter. (a road traveled by foot)

_ _ _ _

Remove one letter. (Addition, subtraction, and multiplication are a part of _____.)

_ _ _ _

Change the first letter. (used to light fires)

_ _ _ _

Change the first letter. (We are going to a pumpkin _____ to pick pumpkins.)

_ _ _ _

Add one letter. (worn on the wrist to help you tell time)

_ _ _ _

Add one letter. (_____ do you want to eat tonight?)

hat

Pirate Word Ladders

Name: _____

Directions - Read the clues and write each word on the ladder. Start at the bottom and climb to the top of the ladder.

Add a letter. (to judge the quality of someone or something)

_ _ _ _ _

Rearrange the letters. (a small rodent)

_ _ _ _

Remove two letters. (Drawing and painting are both done in an _____ class.)

_ _ _ _

Rearrange the letters and add a "t" at the end. (A person who knows a lot is _____.)

_ _ _ _ _

Remove the first letter and add one letter at the end. (a part of your body)

_ _ _ _ _

Change the first letter. (Pigs, cows, and goats can all live on a _____.)

_ _ _ _ _

warm

Name: _____

Pirate Word Ladders

Directions - Read the clues and write each word on the ladder. Start at the bottom and climb to the top of the ladder.

_ _ _ _ _ _

Change the last letter. (another word for a tale)

_ _ _ _ _ _

Change the last letter. (there may be lightning and thunder)

_ _ _ _ _ _

Add a letter. (a place where you buy things)

_ _ _ _ _

Change the first letter. (past tense of tear)

_ _ _ _ _

Add a letter at the end. (something toward the front, ex. _____head, _____arm)

_ _ _ _

Remove the last three letters. (What did you do that _____?)

forest

Pirate Word Ladders

Name: _____

Directions - Read the clues and write each word on the ladder. Start at the bottom and climb to the top of the ladder.

Remove the last word. (You can _____ it!)

_ _

Change the contraction into it's long form.

_ _ _ _

Change the vowel. (a contraction)

_ _ _ _ '

Change the first letter. (a dip or impression in a flat surface)

_ _ _ _

Change the vowel. (A penny is worth one _____.)

_ _ _ '

Make can not a contraction.

_ _ _ _ '

can not

Name: _____

Pirate Word Ladders

Directions - Read the clues and write each word on the ladder. Start at the bottom and climb to the top of the ladder.

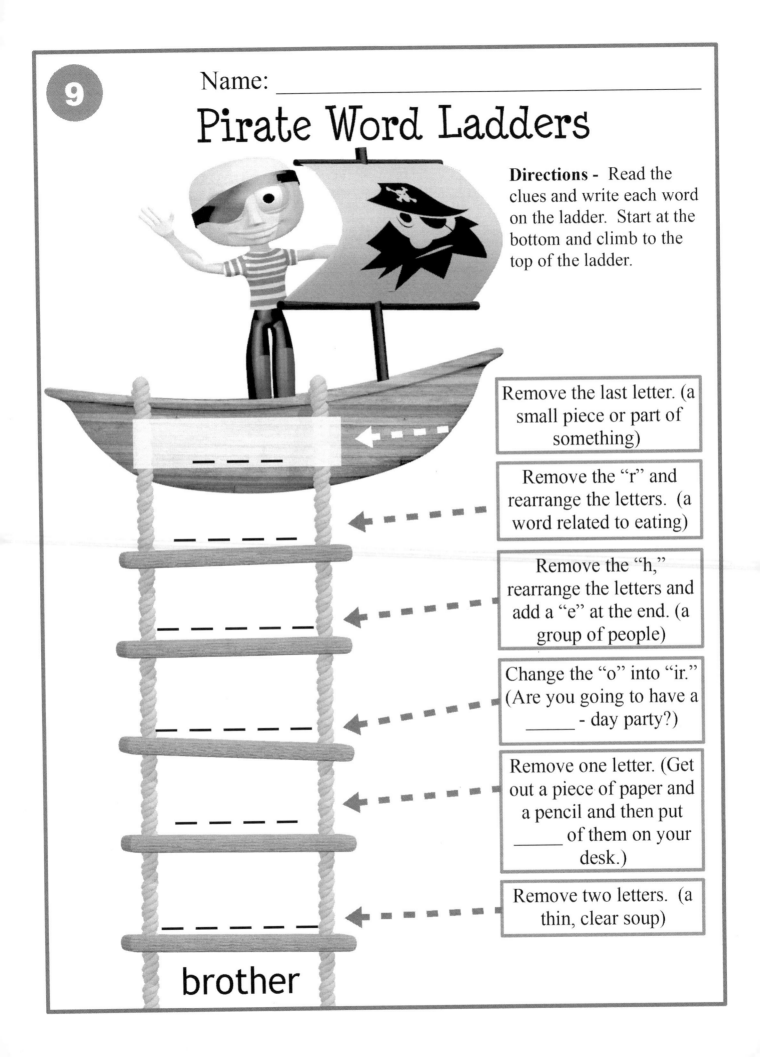

_ _ _ _

Remove the last letter. (a small piece or part of something)

_ _ _ _

Remove the "r" and rearrange the letters. (a word related to eating)

_ _ _ _ _

Remove the "h," rearrange the letters and add a "e" at the end. (a group of people)

_ _ _ _

Change the "o" into "ir." (Are you going to have a _____ - day party?)

_ _ _ _

Remove one letter. (Get out a piece of paper and a pencil and then put _____ of them on your desk.)

_ _ _ _ _

Remove two letters. (a thin, clear soup)

brother

Name: _____

Pirate Word Ladders

Directions - Read the clues and write each word on the ladder. Start at the bottom and climb to the top of the ladder.

_ _ _ _ _

Make the word plural. (Remember to change the "y.")

_ _ _ _ _

Add a letter at the end. (a magical creature)

_ _ _ _ _

Change the first letter. (another word for beautiful)

_ _ _ _ _

Make the word singular.

_ _ _ _ _

Remove one letter. (these are on your head)

_ _ _ _ _

Make chair plural.

chair

Name: _____

Pirate Word Ladders

Directions - Read the clues and write each word on the ladder. Start at the bottom and climb to the top of the ladder.

Make the word plural. (Remember to change the "y.")

Remove the first letter and add two. (a small red fruit)

Make the word singular.

Change one of the "b's" into a doubled letter. (something bears like to eat)

Make the word plural. (Remember to change the "y.")

Add a letter. (a very young child)

bay

Name: _____

Pirate Word Ladders

Directions - Read the clues and write each word on the ladder. Start at the bottom and climb to the top of the ladder.

Change one letter. (Johnny _____ when he is sad.)

Make the word plural. (James likes to eat French - _____.)

Change the second letter. (a way to cook)

Make the word singular.

Change the first letter. (plural- small flying insects)

Drop the "y" and add "ies."

try

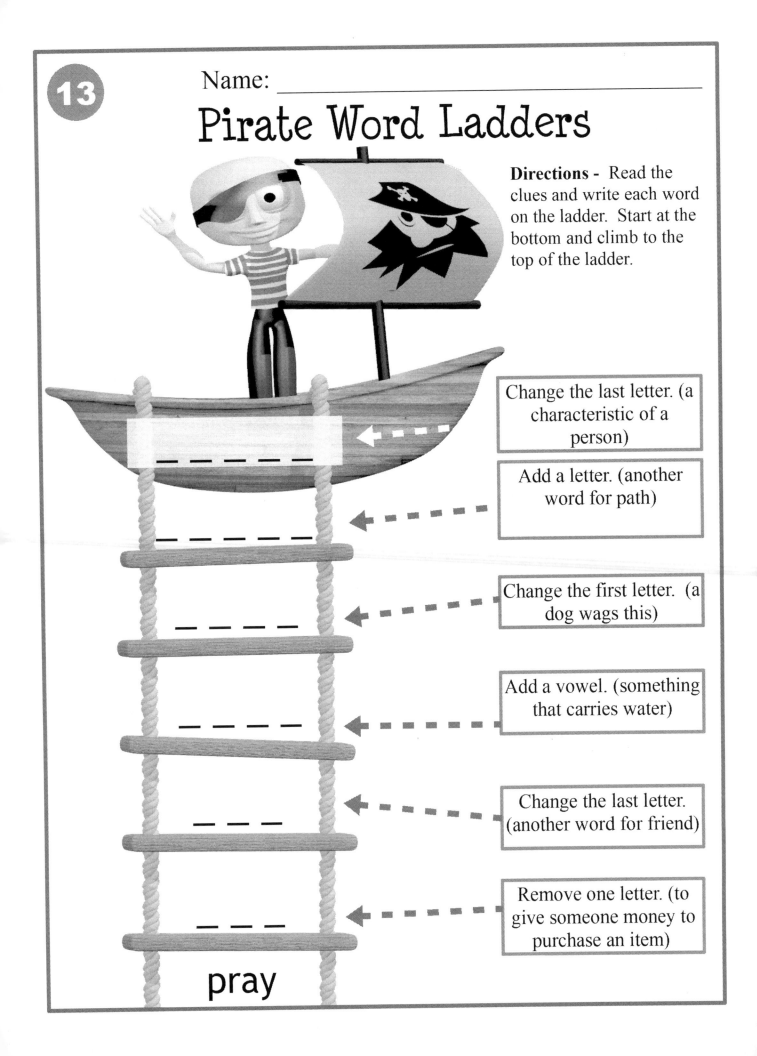

Name: _____

Pirate Word Ladders

Directions - Read the clues and write each word on the ladder. Start at the bottom and climb to the top of the ladder.

Change the last letter. (a characteristic of a person)

Add a letter. (another word for path)

Change the first letter. (a dog wags this)

Add a vowel. (something that carries water)

Change the last letter. (another word for friend)

Remove one letter. (to give someone money to purchase an item)

pray

Name: _____

Pirate Word Ladders

Directions - Read the clues and write each word on the ladder. Start at the bottom and climb to the top of the ladder.

Change the first letter. (to smell bad)

_ _ _ _

Change the last letter. (seven days)

_ _ _ _

Remove a letter. (another word for cry)

_ _ _

Change the last letter. (you do this with a broom)

_ _ _ _

Change one of the vowels. (Cookies, cake, and candy all taste _____.)

_ _ _ _

Add a letter. (a liquid that comes out of your skin)

_ _ _ _ _

seat

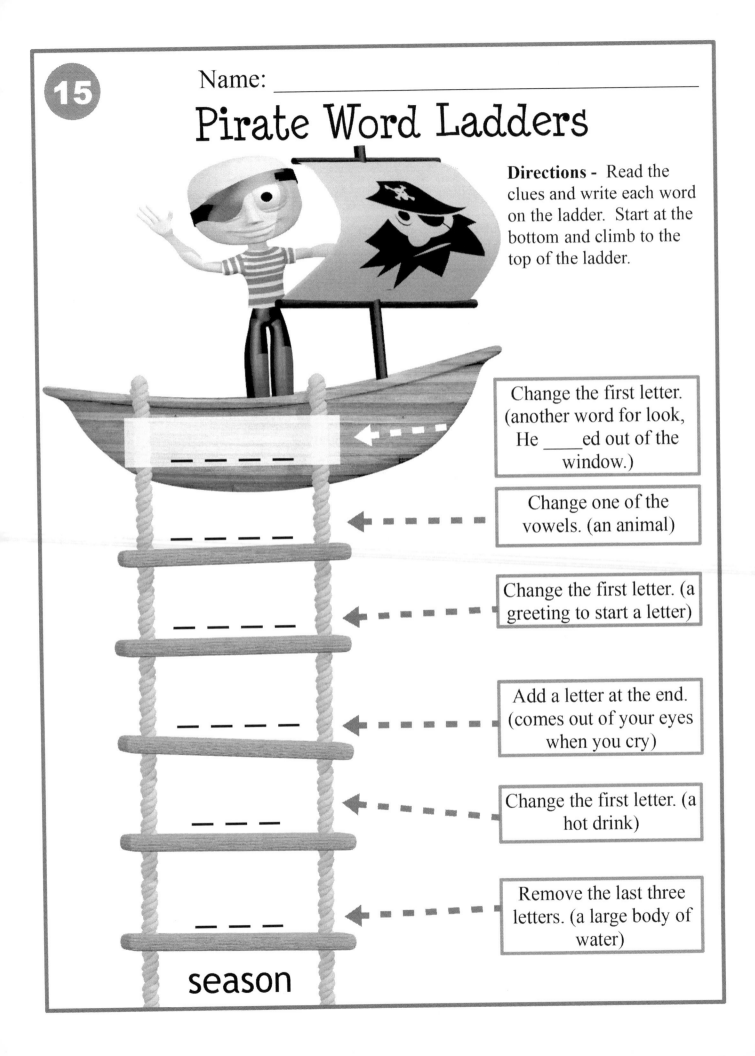

15

Name: _____

Pirate Word Ladders

Directions - Read the clues and write each word on the ladder. Start at the bottom and climb to the top of the ladder.

_ _ _ _ _

Change the first letter. (another word for look, He ____ed out of the window.)

_ _ _ _ _

Change one of the vowels. (an animal)

_ _ _ _ _

Change the first letter. (a greeting to start a letter)

_ _ _ _ _

Add a letter at the end. (comes out of your eyes when you cry)

_ _ _ _

Change the first letter. (a hot drink)

_ _ _

Remove the last three letters. (a large body of water)

season

Name: _____

Pirate Word Ladders

Directions - Read the clues and write each word on the ladder. Start at the bottom and climb to the top of the ladder.

_ _ _ _ _

Add a letter. (a hard protective covering for an animal)

_ _ _ _

Change the first letter. (to give something in exchange for money)

_ _ _

Remove the last two letters. (another word for shout)

_ _ _ _

Change the first letter. (a color)

_ _ _ _ _

Change one of the vowels. (another word for friend)

_ _ _ _ _

Change the first letter. (When walking in line you must _____ the person in front of you.)

hollow

Name: _____

Pirate Word Ladders

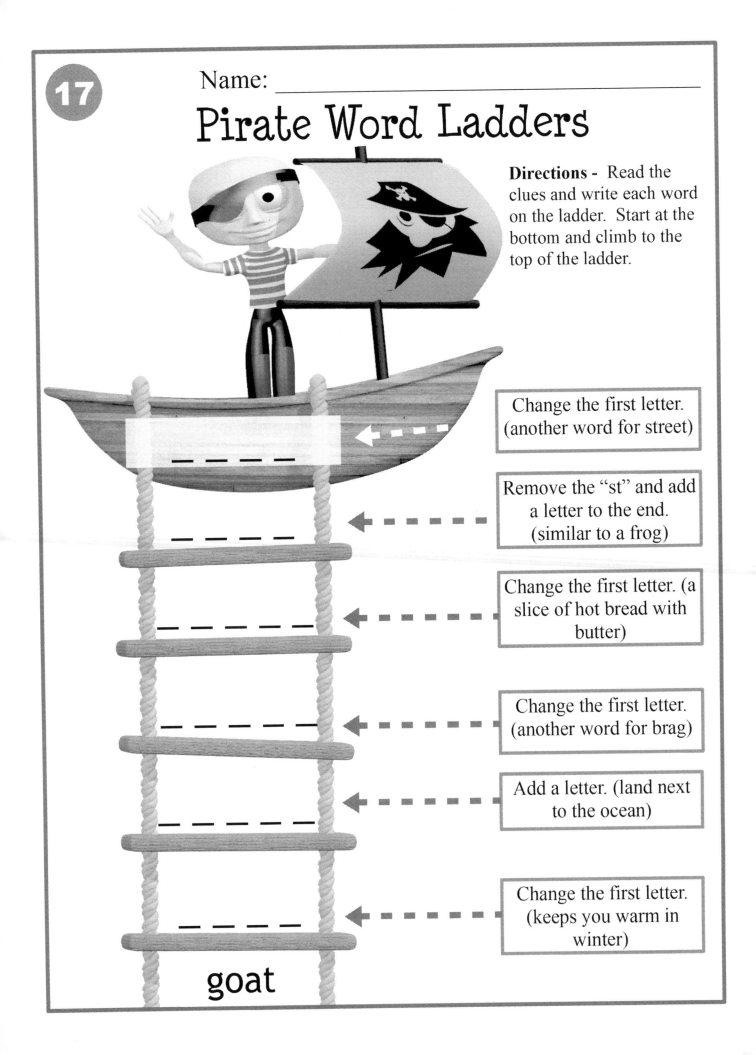

Directions - Read the clues and write each word on the ladder. Start at the bottom and climb to the top of the ladder.

Change the first letter. (another word for street)

Remove the "st" and add a letter to the end. (similar to a frog)

Change the first letter. (a slice of hot bread with butter)

Change the first letter. (another word for brag)

Add a letter. (land next to the ocean)

Change the first letter. (keeps you warm in winter)

goat

Name: _____

Pirate Word Ladders

Directions - Read the clues and write each word on the ladder. Start at the bottom and climb to the top of the ladder.

_ _ _ _ ← Change the first two letters. (not dead)

_ _ _ _ ← Add a letter. (to operate a car or other vehicle)

_ _ _ _ ← Change a letter. (to jump into the water head first)

_ _ _ _ ← Change the first letter. (to eat dinner)

_ _ _ ← Add a letter. (We must _____ up to get ready to go to PE.)

_ _ _ ← Change the first letter. (not the truth)

pie

Name: _____

Pirate Word Ladders

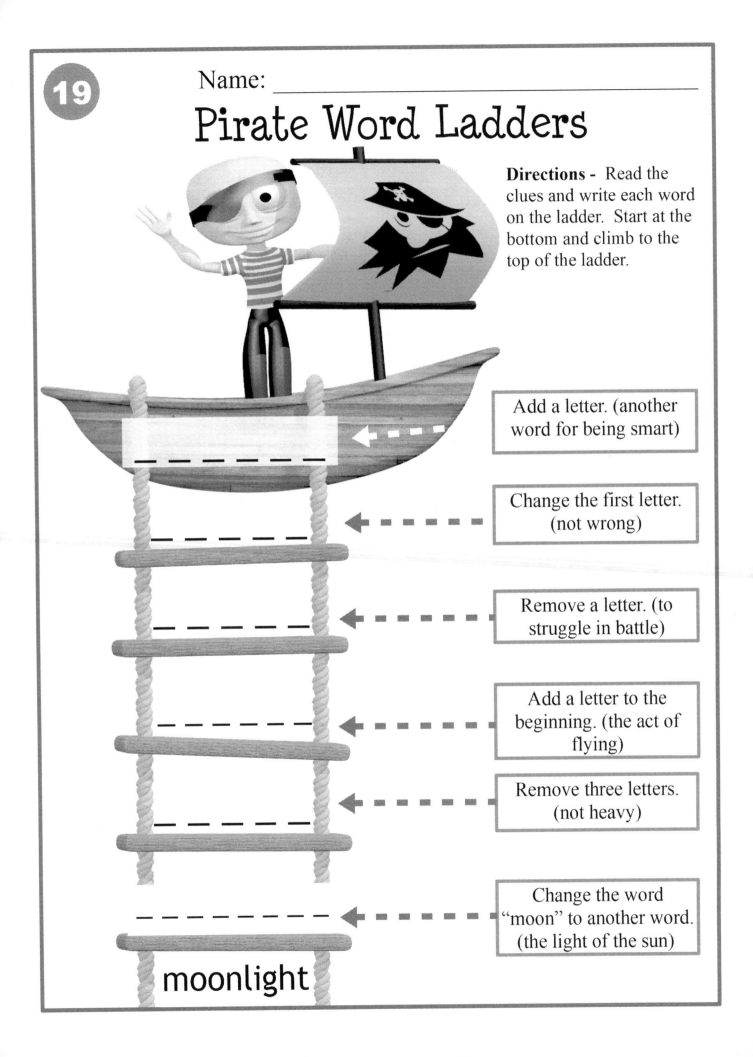

Directions - Read the clues and write each word on the ladder. Start at the bottom and climb to the top of the ladder.

Add a letter. (another word for being smart)

Change the first letter. (not wrong)

Remove a letter. (to struggle in battle)

Add a letter to the beginning. (the act of flying)

Remove three letters. (not heavy)

Change the word "moon" to another word. (the light of the sun)

moonlight

Pirate Word Ladders

Name: _____

Directions - Read the clues and write each word on the ladder. Start at the bottom and climb to the top of the ladder.

Change the letter "g." (a shelf above the fireplace)

Change the first letter. (to ruin or spoil something)

Change the "ck" into two other letters. (hair can get these)

Change the vowel. (football players do this)

Change the "n." (might make you giggle)

Remove the "wr" and add a letter at the beginning. (the sound of small bells.)

wrinkle

Name: _____

Pirate Word Ladders

Directions - Read the clues and write each word on the ladder. Start at the bottom and climb to the top of the ladder.

Change the first "t." (a large building with stone walls and towers)

Change the first letter. (a group of cows)

Change the first letter. (a fight between armies)

Change the double letters and change the "i" to an "a." (babies play with these)

Change the first letter. (another word for a puzzle)

Change the double letters. (another word for violin)

fizzle

Name: _____

Pirate Word Ladders

22

Directions - Read the clues and write each word on the ladder. Start at the bottom and climb to the top of the ladder.

Change the first letter. (another word for see)

Remove a letter. (something you read)

Change the last letter. (another word for stream)

Change the first letter. (used to sweep the floor)

Add a letter to the beginning. (a person in charge of a horse or a man about to get married)

Remove the "mushy" stuff. (a part of a house)

mushroom

Name: _____

Pirate Word Ladders

Directions - Read the clues and write each word on the ladder. Start at the bottom and climb to the top of the ladder.

_ _ _ _ _

Remove the first letter and add two. (not rough)

_ _ _ _ _

Remove the last letter and add two. (something that is in your mouth)

_ _ _ _ _

Change the first letter. (an object that makes it easier to do a job)

_ _ _ _

Change the middle two letters so that the word sounds the same as the one before. (another word for idiot)

_ _ _ _

Change the first letter. (when you've eaten as much as you can)

_ _ _ _

Remove the "sh" and add double letters. (the opposite of push)

push

Pirate Word Ladders

Directions - Read the clues and write each word on the ladder. Start at the bottom and climb to the top of the ladder.

Change the first letter. (an expression used to express admiration)

Remove the first letter. (to move a boat with oars)

Remove the last letter. (when you get bigger)

Remove the "f" and add two letters. (a deep sound that animals make)

Rearrange the letters. (another word for bird)

Remove the "er." (to move in a stream)

flower

Name: _____

Pirate Word Ladders

Directions - Read the clues and write each word on the ladder. Start at the bottom and climb to the top of the ladder.

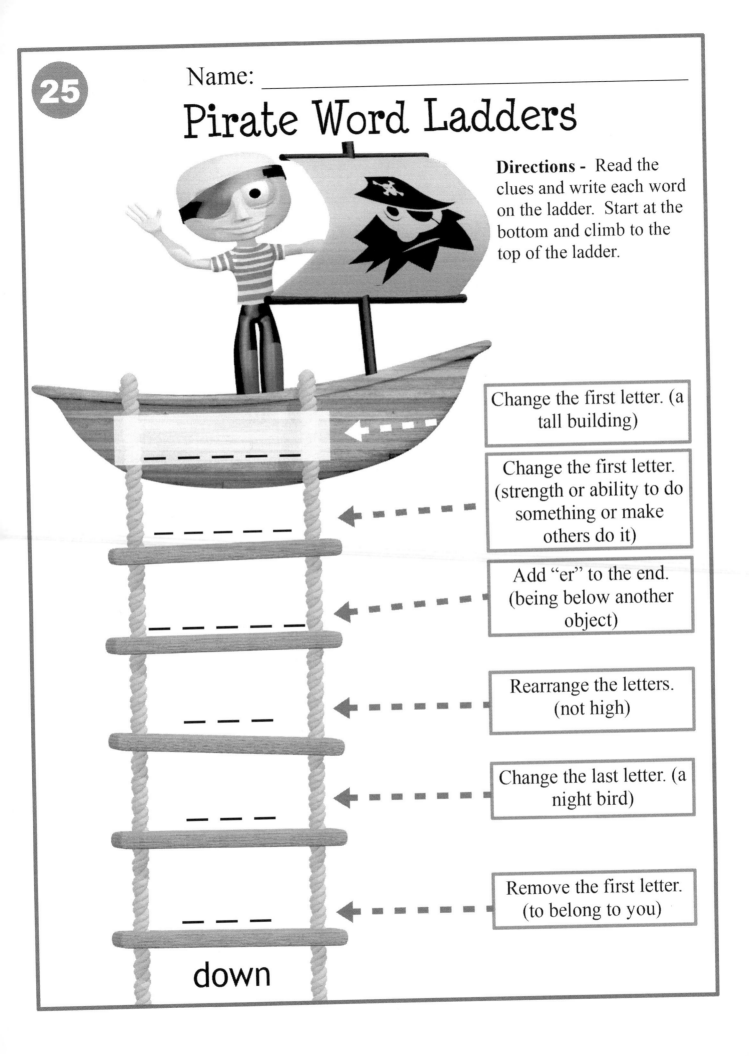

Change the first letter. (a tall building)

Change the first letter. (strength or ability to do something or make others do it)

Add "er" to the end. (being below another object)

Rearrange the letters. (not high)

Change the last letter. (a night bird)

Remove the first letter. (to belong to you)

down

Pirate Word Ladders

Directions - Read the clues and write each word on the ladder. Start at the bottom and climb to the top of the ladder.

_ _ _ _

Change the first letter. (makes things stick together)

_ _ _ _ _

Remove the "ew" and add two vowels at the end. The word will sound the same as the one before. (a color)

_ _ _ _

Change the first letter. (past tense of blow)

_ _ _ _ _

Change one letter. (past tense of slay)

_ _ _ _

Remove the vowels and add "ew" at the end. (another word for soup)

_ _ _ _ _

Remove the "fr" and add a letter at the beginning. (a set of clothes worn for special occasions)

fruit

Name: _____

Pirate Word Ladders

Directions - Read the clues and write each word on the ladder. Start at the bottom and climb to the top of the ladder.

Remove the "b" and add two letters at the beginning. (do something in a glad way)

Add two letters at the end. (do something in a bad way)

Change the first letter. (not good)

Remove the "ly." (not happy)

Remove the "oft" and add two letters in the middle. (do something in a sad way)

Add "ly" to the end to make it an adverb. (do something in a soft way)

soft

Pirate Word Ladders

Directions - Read the clues and write each word on the ladder. Start at the bottom and climb to the top of the ladder.

_ _ _ _ _ _ _

Add "ful" to the end. (full of dread)

_ _ _ _ _

Change the last letter. (to fear greatly)

_ _ _ _ _

Remove the "t" and add two letters. (you have these when you are asleep)

_ _ _ _

Change the last letter. (a group of people working towards the same goal)

_ _ _ _

Remove the "ful." (comes out of your eyes when crying)

_ _ _ _ _

Change the first letter. (full of tears)

fearful

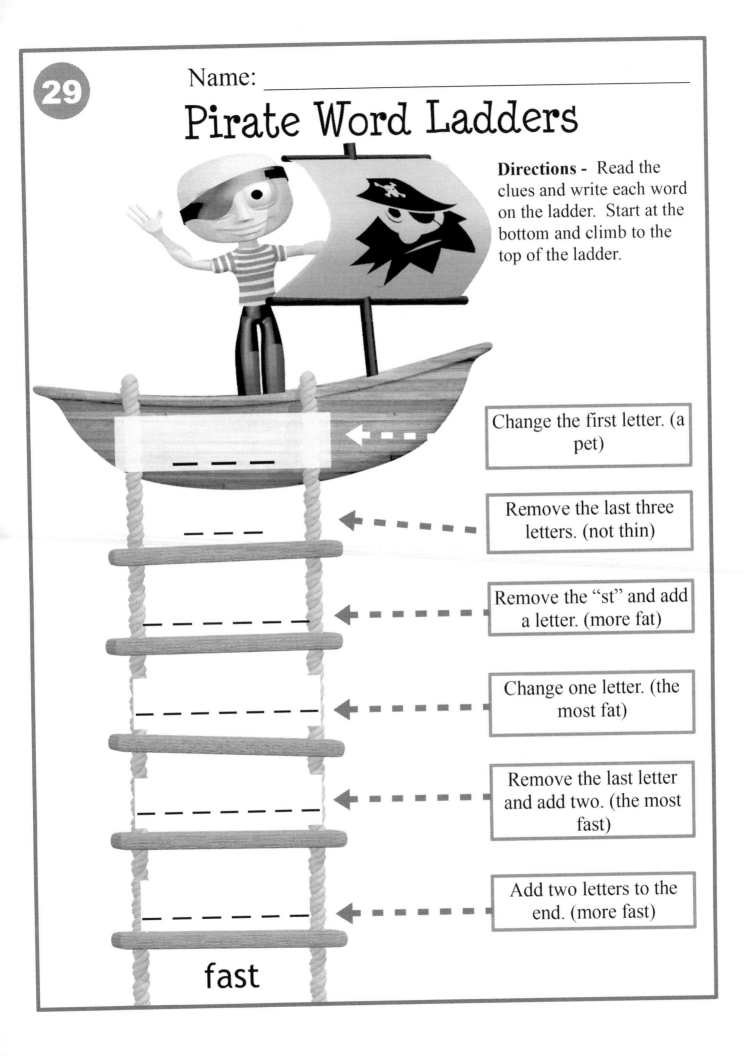

Name: _____

Pirate Word Ladders

Directions - Read the clues and write each word on the ladder. Start at the bottom and climb to the top of the ladder.

_ _ _

Change the first letter. (a pet)

_ _ _

Remove the last three letters. (not thin)

_ _ _ _

Remove the "st" and add a letter. (more fat)

_ _ _ _ _

Change one letter. (the most fat)

_ _ _ _ _

Remove the last letter and add two. (the most fast)

_ _ _ _

Add two letters to the end. (more fast)

fast

Pirate Word Ladders

Directions - Read the clues and write each word on the ladder. Start at the bottom and climb to the top of the ladder.

_____ (Remove the last two letters. (not short))

_____ Remove the "st" and add a letter. (more tall)

_____ Remove the "sm" and add one letter. (the most tall)

_____ Remove the last letter and add two. (the most small)

_____ Add two letters at the end. (more small)

_____ Add one letter. (not big)

mall

Name: _____

Pirate Word Ladders

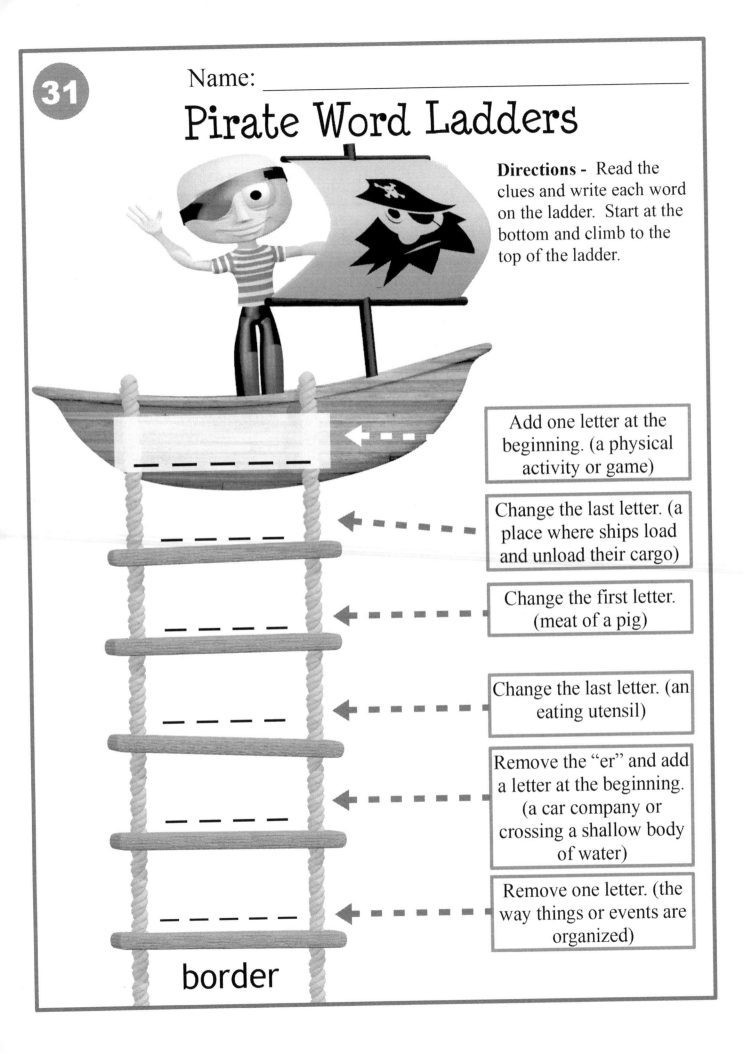

Directions - Read the clues and write each word on the ladder. Start at the bottom and climb to the top of the ladder.

Add one letter at the beginning. (a physical activity or game)

Change the last letter. (a place where ships load and unload their cargo)

Change the first letter. (meat of a pig)

Change the last letter. (an eating utensil)

Remove the "er" and add a letter at the beginning. (a car company or crossing a shallow body of water)

Remove one letter. (the way things or events are organized)

border

Name: _____

Pirate Word Ladders

Directions - Read the clues and write each word on the ladder. Start at the bottom and climb to the top of the ladder.

_ _ _ _ _ _ ← Add two letters at the beginning. (not honest or unequal)

_ _ _ _ _ ← Add a vowel. (another word for just or equal treatment)

_ _ _ _ ← Change the last letter. (a type of tree that is used during Christmas time)

_ _ _ ← Remove one letter. (part of a fish)

_ _ _ _ ← Change the first letter. (locate something that is lost)

_ _ _ _ ← Remove the first two letters. (another word for nice)

unkind

Name: _____

Pirate Word Ladders

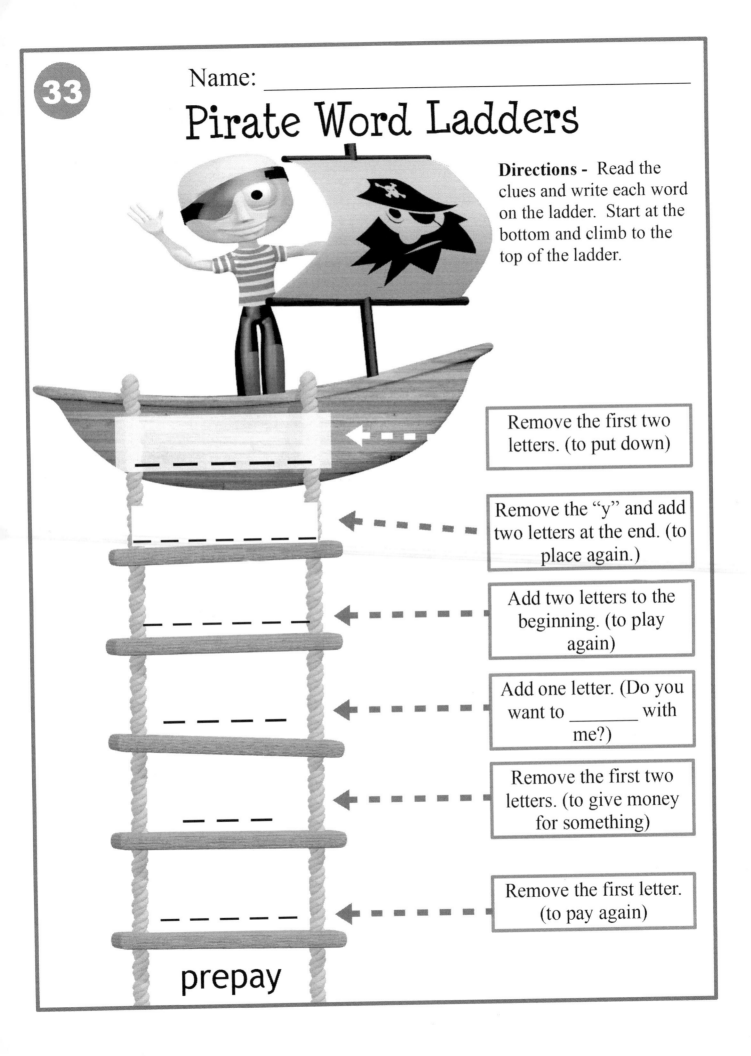

Directions - Read the clues and write each word on the ladder. Start at the bottom and climb to the top of the ladder.

Remove the first two letters. (to put down)

Remove the "y" and add two letters at the end. (to place again.)

Add two letters to the beginning. (to play again)

Add one letter. (Do you want to _____ with me?)

Remove the first two letters. (to give money for something)

Remove the first letter. (to pay again)

prepay

Pirate Word Ladders

Directions - Read the clues and write each word on the ladder. Start at the bottom and climb to the top of the ladder.

_ _ _ _

Change the last letter. (to be aware of something)

_ _ _ _

Change the last letter. (a round handle)

_ _ _ _

Change the vowel. (another word for tangle)

_ _ _ _

Remove the "f" and add two letters. (type of needlework using yarn)

_ _ _

Change the vowel. (in good shape)

_ _ _

Remove the last letter. (not thin)

fate

Pirate Word Ladders

Name: _____

Directions - Read the clues and write each word on the ladder. Start at the bottom and climb to the top of the ladder.

Change the "li" into two different letters. (Small pieces of cake left over are called _____(s.)

Add a letter at the beginning. (to move yourself up higher)

Change the vowel. (an arm or leg)

Change the last letter. (an animal)

Change the first letter. (having a limb that doesn't work well)

Add a letter at the end. (not different)

Sam

Pirate Word Ladders

Directions - Read the clues and write each word on the ladder. Start at the bottom and climb to the top of the ladder.

_ _ _ _

Change the first letter. (a long loud breath)

_ _ _ _

Remove the "t" and add two letters at the end. (not low)

_ _ _

Change the vowel. (Steven ___ the ball with a bat.)

_ _ _

Remove the first and last letters. (not cold)

_ _ _ _

Change the last two letters. (a picture taken with a camera)

_ _ _ _ _

Remove the first two letters, change the "a" to an "o," and add a letter at the end. (used to make calls.)

orphan

Name: _____

Pirate Word Ladders

Directions - Read the clues and write each word on the ladder. Start at the bottom and climb to the top of the ladder.

Remove the last two letters and add one. Remember to capitalize. (a boy's name)

Change the "w" into a "u" and add a letter at the end. (a temporary stop, the word will sound the same.)

Add a letter at the end. (make the word plural)

Remove the first two letters and add one. (the foot or hand of an animal)

Change the first two letters. (when frozen things melt)

Remove the "r" and rearrange the letters. (sharp curved nail of an animal)

crawl

Pirate Word Ladders

Directions - Read the clues and write each word on the ladder. Start at the bottom and climb to the top of the ladder.

Remove the first and last letters then add a letter at the beginning. (another word for giggle)

Remove the last two letters and add "ught." (past tense of teach)

Change the first letter. (another word for speak)

Change the last letter. (to go somewhere on foot)

Change the first letter. (the side of a room)

Remove the first letter. (not short)

stall

Name: _____

Pirate Word Ladders

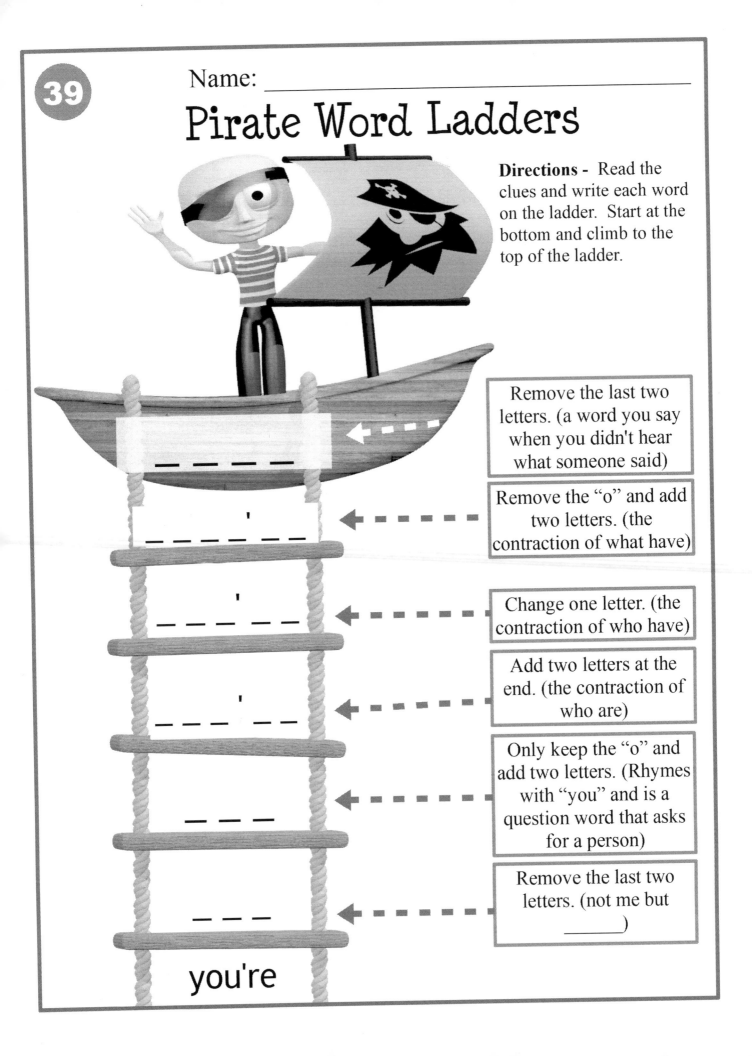

Directions - Read the clues and write each word on the ladder. Start at the bottom and climb to the top of the ladder.

Remove the last two letters. (a word you say when you didn't hear what someone said)

Remove the "o" and add two letters. (the contraction of what have)

Change one letter. (the contraction of who have)

Add two letters at the end. (the contraction of who are)

Only keep the "o" and add two letters. (Rhymes with "you" and is a question word that asks for a person)

Remove the last two letters. (not me but _____)

you're

Pirate Word Ladders

Directions - Read the clues and write each word on the ladder. Start at the bottom and climb to the top of the ladder.

_ _ _ _

Change the first letter. (something that has been mixed)

_ _ _ _ _

Remove the second letter and add two. (A faucet is a bathroom _____.)

_ _ _ _ _

Remove the "ea" and add one letter. (a time to come)

_ _ _ _ _

Add "ure" to the end of the word. (a part or detail that stands out)

_ _ _ _

Change the first letter. (an amazing act or deed)

_ _ _ _

Add one letter at the end. (a piece of furniture that you sit on)

sea

Answer Key

1.
team
tear
fear
pear
peak
sneak
sneakers

2.
string
sting
sling
cling
chin
chick
chicken

3.
sang
song
long
lock
luck
duck
dock

4.
rice
race
rage
sage
space
place
replace

5.
path
math
match
patch
watch
what
hat

6.
rate
rat
art
smart
arms
farm
warm

7.
story
storm
store
tore
fore
for
forest

8.
do
do not
don't
dent
cent
can't
can not

9.
bit
bite
tribe
birth
both
broth
brother

10.
fairies
fairy
fair
hair
hairs
chairs
chair

11.
cherries
cherry
berry
berries
babies
baby
bay

12.
cries
fries
fry
fly
flies
tries
try

13.
trait
trail
tail
pail
pal
pay
pray

14.
reek
week
weep
sweep
sweet
sweat
seat

15.
peer
deer
dear
tear
tea
sea
season

16.
shell
sell
yell
yellow
fellow
follow
hollow

17.
road
toad
toast
boast
coast
coat
goat

18.
alive
drive
dive
dine
line
lie
pie

19.
bright
right
fight
flight
light
sunlight
moonlight

20.
mantle
mangle
tangle
tackle
tickle
tinkle
wrinkle

21.
castle
cattle
battle
rattle
riddle
fiddle
fizzle

22.
look
book
brook
broom
groom
room
mushroom

23.
smooth
tooth
tool
fool
full
pull
push

24.
wow
row
grow
growl
fowl
flow
flower

25.
tower
power
lower
low
owl
own
down

26.
glue
blue
blew
slew
stew
suit
fruit

27.
gladly
badly
bad
sad
sadly
softly
soft

28.
dreadful
dread
dream
team
tear
tearful
fearful

29.
cat
fat
fatter
fattest
fastest
faster
fast

30.
tall
taller
tallest
smallest
smaller
small
mall

31.
sport
port
pork
fork
ford
order
border

32.
unfair
fair
fir
fin
find
kind
unkind

33.
place
replace
replay
play
pay
repay
prepay

34.
know
knob
knot
knit
fit
fat
fate

35.
crumb
climb
limb
lamb
lame
same
Sam

36.
sigh
high
hit
hot
photo
phone
orphan

37.
Paul
pause
paws
paw
thaw
claw
crawl

38.
laugh
taught
talk
walk
wall
tall
stall

39.
what
what've
who've
who're
who
you
you're

40.
mixture
fixture
future
feature
feat
seat
sea

Kaylee's Education Studio

www.kayedstudio.com

Find great teaching resources like:

- worksheets
- games
- classroom management tools
- and many freebies

My first picture book

b and d are buddies

by Brenda Olsen

Available in print and for the Kindle Fire.

Made in the USA
Middletown, DE
06 April 2018